Patterns Around Us

Recognizing Patterns

Tony Hyland

Publishing Credits

Editor
Sara Johnson

Editorial Director
Emily R. Smith, M.A.Ed.

Editor-in-Chief
Sharon Coan, M.S.Ed.

Creative Director
Lee Aucoin

Publisher
Rachelle Cracchiolo, M.S.Ed.

Image Credits

The author and publisher would like to gratefully credit or acknowledge the following for permission to reproduce copyright material: cover Shutterstock; p.1 Shutterstock; p.4 (bottom left) Photolibrary/Alamy; p.4 (top right) iStock; p.5 (left) Shutterstock; p.5 (right) Bigstock; p.6 (top right, bottom left) Shutterstock; p.6 (middle right) iStock; p.7 (top right, bottom right) Shutterstock; p.7 (middle left) Photolibrary.com; p.7 (middle right) Photolibrary.com/Alamy; p.8 Shutterstock; p.9 Photolibrary.com/Alamy; p.12 Shutterstock; p.13 (top) Shutterstock; p.13 (bottom) Photolibrary.com./Alamy; p.18 Photolibrary/Alamy; p.19 Shutterstock; p.20 Shutterstock; p.21 (top) iStock; p.21 (bottom) M. C. Escher Company; p.22 iStock; p.23 Photolibrary.com/Alamy; p.24 Getty Images; p.25 Alamy; p.26 Shutterstock; p.27 (top) Alamy; p.27 (bottom) Corbis; p.28 Photolibrary.com.

While every care has been taken to trace and acknowledge copyright, the publishers tender their apologies for any accidental infringement where copyright has proved untraceable. They would be pleased to come to a suitable arrangement with the rightful owner in each case.

Teacher Created Materials

5301 Oceanus Drive
Huntington Beach, CA 92649-1030
http://www.tcmpub.com
ISBN 978-0-7439-0895-5
© 2009 Teacher Created Materials, Inc.
Reprinted 2013

Table of Contents

What Is a Pattern?

A pattern is something that is **repeated**. A pattern can be a repeated **design**. Many clothes have patterns. A pattern can also be something that is used over and over again, like a dress pattern.

These paper clothing patterns will be used to make many clothes.

If you look around, you will see patterns in all sorts of places. There are patterns in nature and in buildings. There are patterns in numbers. Even the desks in your classroom may form a pattern.

monarch butterfly

LET'S EXPLORE MATH

Look at this number pattern: 1, 6, 11, 16, __, __

a. What numbers come next in this pattern?

Now look at this number pattern: 1, 4, 8, 13, 19, __

b. What number comes next in this pattern?

c. What numbers did you add to work out your answer?

Patterns in Nature

There are many patterns in nature. Plants can be **recognized** by their leaf shapes and the **vein** patterns on their leaves. Look at these leaves. The patterns are different for each kind of tree.

Even flower petals are in patterns. Daisies have long narrow petals that form circles.

maple leaves

birch leaves

daisies

Animal Patterns

Many animals have patterns on their bodies. Bees have striped patterns. Butterflies and moths have patterns on their wings. Leopards have spotted patterns. Their spots are used as **camouflage** (KAM-uh-flazh) in the long grass.

bee

leopard

regal moth

Zebras have black and white stripes. Zebras can recognize each other because the striped patterns are different on each animal!

zebras

Patterns in Rocks

Rocks often show patterns. Layers of rock build up over millions of years. These layers are called strata (STRAH-tuh). The pattern of the different strata can be seen on cliff faces.

At the Grand Canyon, in Arizona, you can see many layers of strata. Each layer of rock is a different color. The layers form striped patterns in the cliff faces. Scientists study these patterns. Some layers show that the area was once a shallow sea. Other layers show that the area was a swamp or a desert.

Strata Patterns

If you put information about the Grand Canyon strata into a graph, you can easily see when the layers were formed and the name of each strata.

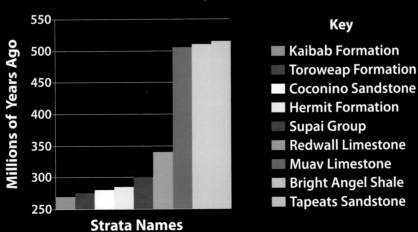

Grand Canyon Strata Age

Millions of Years Ago

Strata Names

Key

- Kaibab Formation
- Toroweap Formation
- Coconino Sandstone
- Hermit Formation
- Supai Group
- Redwall Limestone
- Muav Limestone
- Bright Angel Shale
- Tapeats Sandstone

Geometric Patterns

Geometric patterns are easy to make. Repeating just one shape makes a simple pattern. You can make the pattern look different by changing colors. You can also use different shapes.

Flips and Turns

You can even change the positions of the shapes by flipping or turning them. This is called **transformation**. Transforming a shape, such as turning or flipping it, makes a more **complex** pattern.

Turning, or rotating, a shape makes another pattern. The shape can be turned a ¼, ½, or ¾ turn at a time.

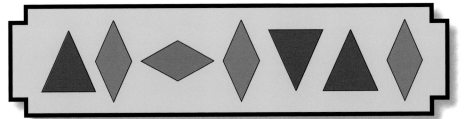

Reflection patterns are made by reversing, or flipping, a shape to make a mirror image of it.

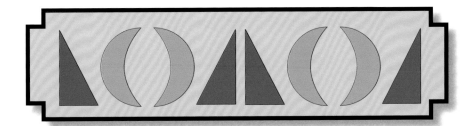

LET'S EXPLORE MATH

a. Look at the pattern above. What shape belongs on the line?

b. Look at the pattern above. Which two shapes belong on the lines?

Tiling Patterns

People have used tiles to make patterns for thousands of years. These patterns are **tessellations**. A tessellation is a pattern that covers a space. There are no overlaps or gaps between the shapes. **Polygons** are used for these types of patterns.

Ancient Patterns!

The word tessellation comes from *tessella*, the Latin word for tile. These patterns have been used for about 6,000 years. These days, you can often see tessellations on floors or walls.

Squares, triangles, and hexagons are the only shapes that fit neatly together by themselves in tessellations. Circles will not fit the pattern unless other shapes are added to fill the gaps.

In some tessellations, the patterns are inside a shape such as a square. This is repeated over and over again. Other tessellations have **symmetrical** patterns.

Repeated hexagons in this honeycomb make a tessellation.

These tiles show a repeated square tessellation.

Number Patterns

Our system of numbers is based on patterns in groups of 10. We count from 1 to 10, and then repeat the numbers in more sets of 10, then in sets of 100, then sets of 1,000, and so on. No matter how far we count, the same pattern of numbers keeps appearing.

1	2	3	4	5	6	7	8	9	10
10	20	30	40	50	60	70	80	90	100
100	200	300	400	500	600	700	800	900	1,000
1,000	2,000	3,000	4,000	5,000	6,000	7,000	8,000	9,000	10,000

Hundred Chart

We can see many patterns in a grid of 100 numbers. If we count by 10s, we get a **vertical** pattern on the grid. Counting by 9s makes a **diagonal** pattern, moving from right to left.

0	1	2	3	4	5	6	7	8	9
10	11	12	13	14	15	16	17	18	19
20	21	22	23	24	25	26	27	28	29
30	31	32	33	34	35	36	37	38	39
40	41	42	43	44	45	46	47	48	49
50	51	52	53	54	55	56	57	58	59
60	61	62	63	64	65	66	67	68	69
70	71	72	73	74	75	76	77	78	79
80	81	82	83	84	85	86	87	88	89
90	91	92	93	94	95	96	97	98	99

LET'S EXPLORE MATH

Look at the hundred chart above.

a. What number do you count by to make a diagonal pattern going from left to right, starting at 0?

b. Start at 0 and count by 2s. Write down all of the numbers. Then count by 4s. Write down all of the numbers. Then count by 8s. Write down all of the numbers. For each sequence, stop as close to 100 as possible.

c. What numbers are in all three counting patterns?

15

Patterns in Multiples

Numbers make many patterns. It is easy to multiply by 9s if you know there is a pattern. The number in the tens column is always 1 less than the number you are multiplying by. And the sum of the numbers always adds up to 9.

$9 \times 1 = 9$ $(0 + 9 = 9)$

$9 \times 2 = 18$ $(1 + 8 = 9)$

$9 \times 3 = 27$ $(2 + 7 = 9)$

$9 \times 4 = 36$ $(3 + 6 = 9)$

$9 \times 5 = 45$ $(4 + 5 = 9)$

$9 \times 6 = 54$ $(5 + 4 = 9)$

$9 \times 7 = 63$ $(6 + 3 = 9)$

$9 \times 8 = 72$ $(7 + 2 = 9)$

$9 \times 9 = 81$ $(8 + 1 = 9)$

$9 \times 10 = 90$ $(9 + 0 = 9)$

Can you find any other interesting patterns in this list of numbers?

Number Sequences

Sequences (SEE-kwen-sez) are also patterns. Number sequences follow a **rule**. Look at this number line. The rule of this sequence is "add 3."

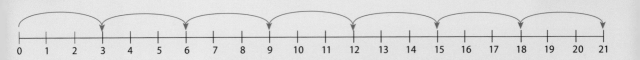

3 + 3 + 3 . . .

If you count by 3s, the digits in each number always add up to 3, 6, or 9. Get a pencil and some paper and check it out for yourself.

LET'S EXPLORE MATH

Draw this number line and answer the questions.

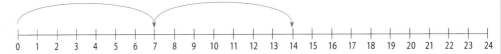

a. What rule is this sequence following?

b. What is the next number in the sequence?

c. Is the number 24 in this sequence?

Patterns in Building

Architects (AR-kuh-tekts) use many shapes to design buildings. Rooms are often square shaped. Doors and windows are rectangles. Bricks and tiles are also many shapes. They can form patterns. Sometimes, patterns are made to decorate the **facade** (fuh-SAHD).

The San Remo apartments in New York City

Architects often design buildings with sets of columns and arches. These can form patterns that decorate the building.

The arches in the Colosseum (ko-luh-SEE-uhm) in Rome create a continuous pattern around the building.

LET'S EXPLORE MATH

Architects also use windows to create patterns on buildings. Draw the table and answer the questions.

a. What are the missing numbers in the table?

b. What is the rule for the number pattern in the table?

Number of Windows on Each Story of the Building

Story	Windows
2	6
3	9
4	

Patterns in Art

Artists have used patterns in paintings and other works of art for thousands of years. Patterns are often used to add interest to pictures.

This Egyptian artwork has many different patterns forming the border that frames the picture.

Some forms of art have patterns that have special meaning. Look at this ancient **Celtic** (KEL-tik) art. The spiral pattern stands for the sun.

Some artists use patterns to make artwork more interesting. In the picture below, the pattern on the field continues into the sky.

M. C. Escher used pictures to create complex patterns that look **three-dimensional**.

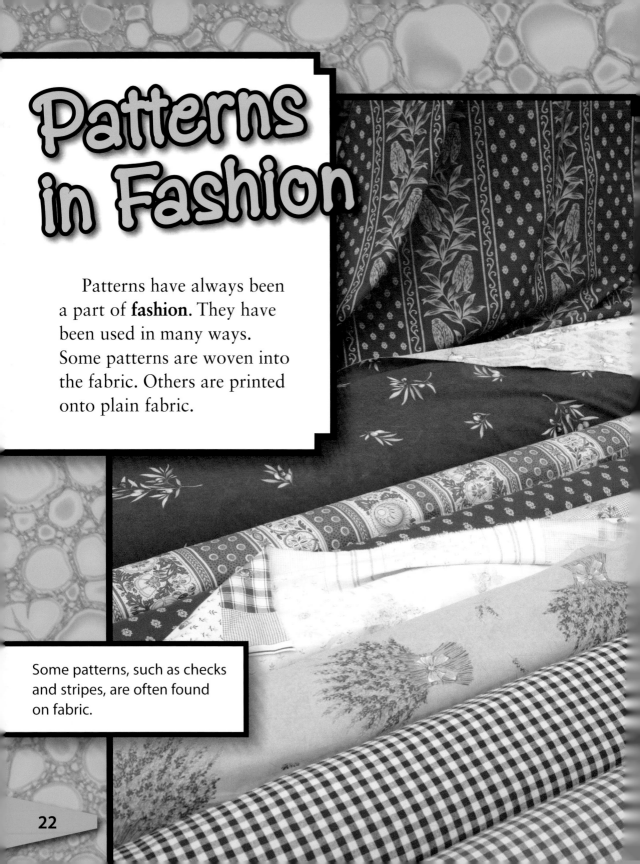

Patterns in Fashion

Patterns have always been a part of **fashion**. They have been used in many ways. Some patterns are woven into the fabric. Others are printed onto plain fabric.

Some patterns, such as checks and stripes, are often found on fabric.

Clothes are cut and made using patterns based on sizes. Patterns for children's clothes are made according to age: 2, 4, 6, 8, up to 16. Patterns for adults are made according to body shapes and sizes. The patterns may be small, medium, or large.

LET'S EXPLORE MATH

The number of pieces of fabric required to make a shirt may depend on the size of the shirt. Draw the table and answer the questions.

a. What are the missing numbers in the table?

b. What is the rule for the number pattern in the table?

Number of Fabric Pieces per Shirt

Shirt	Fabric pieces
1	6
2	12
3	
	24

Patterns in Technology

Many of the machines you see every day are run by computers. Did you know that computers do not use words to tell the machines what to do? Computers use a **binary system**. This is a pattern of 2 numbers: 0 and 1.

This is how you use numbers: 0, 1, 2, 3, 4, and so on. This is how a computer uses numbers: 00000000, 00000001, 00000010, 00000011, 00000100, and so on.

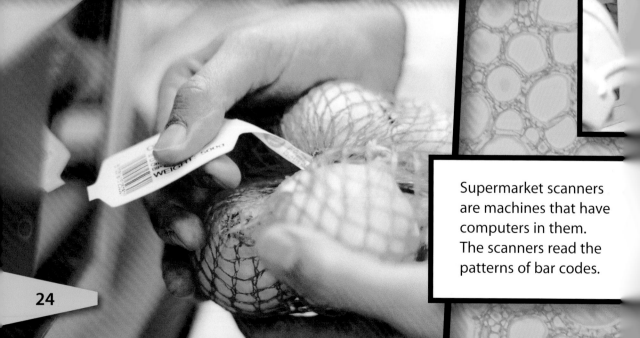

Supermarket scanners are machines that have computers in them. The scanners read the patterns of bar codes.

Making Our Technology

Patterns are also used in factories. A pattern is made for each part of an item. Machines then make thousands of parts by copying each pattern over and over again. Then, the correct number of parts are put together to make complete items.

LET'S EXPLORE MATH

Quick Cars is a car factory. The table shows the number of doors needed to build cars. Draw the table and answer the questions.

a. What are the missing numbers in the table?

b. What is the rule for the number pattern in the table?

Number of Doors Needed

Cars	Doors
2	8
4	16
	24

Patterns in Communication

We use language to talk. Languages use patterns of words and sentences. Different languages use different letters or characters. They also use different sentence patterns. We learn these patterns when we learn to speak.

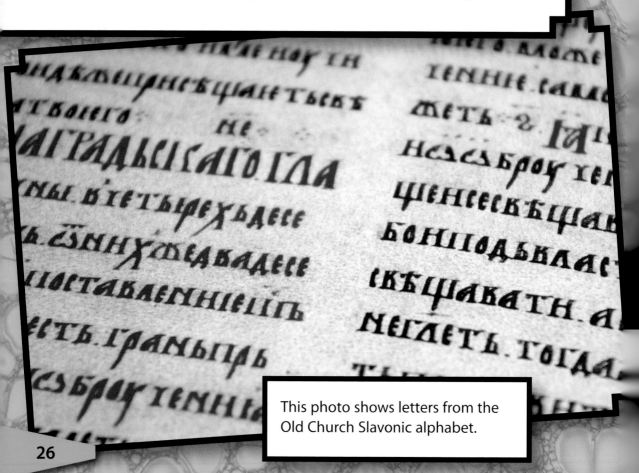

This photo shows letters from the Old Church Slavonic alphabet.

Patterns are all around us. We can see patterns in our cities and in nature. We use number patterns to do mathematics and play games. And when we talk to each other, we talk using patterns!

Famous Fibonacci

The Fibonacci (fee-buh-NAH-chee) sequence is a very famous sequence of numbers. This sequence is named after an Italian math expert, Leonardo Pisano Fibonacci. Fibonacci lived from 1170 to 1250.

Fibonacci numbers are a series of numbers. The numbers follow a special pattern. The first 10 numbers in the Fibonacci sequence are:

1, 1, 2, 3, 5, 8, 13, 21, 34, 55.

Solve It!

Now let's see if you can work out the secret of the Fibonacci sequence. Here's a small clue to help you!

$1 + 1 = 2$

$1 + 2 = 3$

a. What rule does the Fibonacci sequence follow?

b. Continue the addition pattern for the numbers shown above to show how you worked out your answer.

c. What are the next 3 numbers in the sequence after 55?

A Secret Challenge

Now it is your turn to create a secret number code.

d. Work out a number code of your own. Show it to a friend and see if he or she can work out the rule.

Glossary

architects—people who design, or draw, buildings

binary system—a system of numbers that only uses 2 numbers: 0 and 1

camouflage—the act of hiding by having coloring that looks like something else

Celtic—from Brittany, Wales, Ireland, and Scotland

complex—hard to solve

design—a decorative pattern

diagonal—a line that joins two points that are not next to each other or above and below each other

facade—the face, or front, of a building

fashion—the style of clothing that is popular at any given time

geometric—relating to geometry; a part of mathematics that deals with shapes, lines, and angles

polygons—shapes with three or more straight sides

recognized—knew someone or something from before

reflection—a mirror image of something

repeated—done again and again

rule—a statement that is true

sequences—patterns following a rule

symmetrical—having the same size and shape across a line

tessellations—repeating patterns of shapes that fit together with no gaps or overlaps

three-dimensional—having length, width, and height

transformation—changing the way you look at a shape

vein—a channel or tube

vertical—a line that goes straight up and down